MODULE

Measuring and Managing Quality Costs
Version 1.1

AUTHORS:

Shahid Ansari
California State University Northridge

Jan Bell
California State University Northridge

Thomas Klammer
University of North Texas

Carol Lawrence
University of Richmond

Contents
Measuring and Managing Quality Costs

STRATEGIC IMPLICATIONS OF QUALITY COSTS 1
PURPOSE OF THIS MODULE 2
HOW HAS INTEREST IN MEASURING QUALITY COST DEVELOPED? 2
THE NATURE OF QUALITY COSTS 3
THE QUALITY MANAGEMENT SYSTEM 4
   Step 1. Understand Customer Requirements. 4
   Step 2. Establish Quality Goals. 6
   Step 3. Set Work Processes to Meet Quality Goals. 6
   Step 4. Perform Work and Monitor Output. 6
   Step 5. Deliver Product and Monitor Customer Experience. 7
   Step 6. Perform Root Cause Analysis. 7
MEASURING QUALITY COSTS—AN ILLUSTRATION 8
   DFP's Assembly Department Quality Costs. 10
   Firm-Wide Analysis of Quality Costs. 13
USING QUALITY COST DATA TO MANAGE QUALITY 14
   Firm-Wide Spending on Quality. 14
   Spending on Quality by Categories. 14
   Financial Returns from Quality Costs. 15
   Quality Spending and Customer Satisfaction. 17
   Root Cause Analysis of Quality. 20
PROPERTIES OF A QUALITY COST SYSTEM 22
   Technical Attributes of a Quality Cost System. 22
   Behavioral Attributes of a Quality Cost System. 22
   Cultural Attributes of a Quality Cost System. 24
LESSONS LEARNED 24
COMMON TERMS 26
PROBLEMS AND CASES—INTRODUCTORY LEVEL 28
PROBLEMS AND CASES—ADVANCED LEVEL 32
   Case 1: Cascade Seating. 35
   Case 2: Nuclear Safety Research Inc. 37

© The McGraw-Hill Companies, Inc., 1997

All rights reserved. No part of this publication may be reproduced, stored in a retrieval system, or transmitted, in any form or by any means, electronic, mechanical, photocopying, recording, or otherwise, without the prior written permission of the publisher.

ISBN 0-256-27143-7

Printed in the United States of America

0 MZ 3 2 1

Measuring and Managing Quality Cost

DINING IN STYLE WITH ALASKA AIRLINES

Airline passengers can be merciless in their treatment of airlines that do not deliver good service. Northwest Airlines has been called "Northworst." The now-defunct Allegheny Airlines was referred to by New Englanders as "Agony Airlines" due to its cramped seating, which made even short flights uncomfortable.

Alaska Airlines, formerly known as "Elastic Airlines" due to its unreliable, "rubbery" schedules, has successfully overcome its unfortunate label. The airline invested $12 million for guidance equipment to enable its planes to land in low visibility conditions, helping them avoid delays caused by frequent fog in the Northwestern U.S. In order to provide more leg room to passengers, Alaska outfits its planes with 135 seats, while other airlines install 142 to 155 seats in similar planes. Other airlines have reduced their food service to tiny packages of pretzels in order to reduce short-term operating costs. In contrast, Alaska spends more than twice the average of U.S. airlines on food service, serving full course meals which often include fresh salmon or venison. Fresh fruit is available on all Alaska Airlines flights. In a novel touch, the chef routinely visits passengers on board. "It's like I have a restaurant," he says.

Alaska's strategy has worked. The firm was close to bankruptcy in 1971 when new management began the quality movement in the company. By the late 1980s the customer loyalty established over the years helped to protect Alaska Airlines from the devastating profitability declines in the industry. In 1988, when industry profits decreased an average of 169 percent over 1987, Alaska's net income increased by 13 percent. The following year, when profit for air carriers declined an average of 627 percent, to a net loss of $5.122 *billion* per airline, Alaska earned a net income of $17 million.

▲ STRATEGIC IMPLICATIONS OF QUALITY COSTS

Quality costs are costs incurred to ensure that a product or service meets customers' expectations. Alaska Airlines is a good example of a company using spending for quality to gain strategic advantage. The air carrier clearly understands that quality includes not only providing the *features* customers desire, such as seats and meals, but also making certain that these features *perform* at a level expected by customers. It does not just provide a seat, it spends additional money to provide greater leg room. It does not simply serve food, it spends twice as much as other airlines to provide a restaurant-style meal. Clearly, Alaska Airlines feels that extra spending on quality is justified by the strategic benefit provided by meeting or exceeding customers' expectations.

A good system for measuring quality costs is essential for pursuing quality as a strategic goal. In addition, it helps management achieve other strategic goals of producing products at a reasonable cost and delivering a product to customers in a timely fashion.

▲ **Quality.** A well-designed quality costing system supports effective quality management, and so helps a firm compete on the quality dimension of the strategic triangle. As the Alaska Airlines story shows, spending on quality can be an important source of strategic advantage when spending is focused on the aspects of quality most valued by customers.

▲ **Cost.** The total cost of a product includes not only the cost of production, but any additional costs incurred due to quality problems. For a producer, total product cost includes not only manufacturing costs but also costs incurred to fix any defects. For a consumer, the total cost of ownership of a product includes the purchase price and all costs associated with using (owning) a product, including repair and maintenance costs.

▲ **Time.** Improving quality so that we *build quality in,* instead of *inspecting quality in,* avoids nonproductive time spent in inspection, rework, and product recalls. A quality costing system makes the cost of these "non-value-added" activities visible and translates the time savings from eliminating these activities into cost savings.

▲ PURPOSE OF THIS MODULE

This module discusses how to measure and report quality costs to achieve the quality goals of an organization. After reading this module, you should understand:

▲ Why there is greater interest in measuring quality costs today.
▲ The nature of and reasons for measurement of quality costs.
▲ The typical steps in a quality management system.
▲ How to measure quality costs.
▲ How to use cost data to manage quality in an organization.
▲ The technical, behavioral, and cultural properties of a quality costing system.

▲ HOW HAS INTEREST IN MEASURING QUALITY COSTS DEVELOPED?

Contemporary approaches to quality control can be traced to the work of a U.S. engineer named Walter Shewhart and a statistician named W. Edwards Deming. An important contribution of Shewhart and Deming was the use of statistical methods to explain the nature of variation in manufacturing processes. Their focus was on measuring and controlling variation to minimize production of defective units. The approach was to produce first, then check and compare the defect rate against acceptable levels of variation, and to take corrective action only if the variation was more than the prespecified "control interval." In the Shewhart-Deming approach, quality is measured by the number of defects, or products which fall outside the acceptable limits for product variation.

The narrow technical focus to quality measurement was greatly expanded after World War II by Deming, Joseph M. Juran, and Genichi Taguchi. These authors expanded the notion of quality to encompass customer expectations and societal considerations. The cost and benefits of good quality to a producer, to a customer, and to society at large became central concerns. Another important change was to introduce the idea of building quality in rather than inspecting products for defects after production.

In the 1950s, Japanese industry realized it could gain competitive advantage by implementing a modern manufacturing system with no inventory and faster time to market. To do so, however, would require extremely high standards of quality. It turned to Deming for help. His work, along with that of Juran and Taguchi, served as the foundation of the "Total Quality Management" (TQM) movement. The results were extraordinary. In twenty-five short years, Japan transformed itself from a war ravaged nation into an industrial powerhouse. Its reputation for producing quality products gained it a sizable world market share in many industries previously dominated by U.S. and European companies.

U.S. industry got a "wake up call" in the 1980s as firms in industries such as consumer electronics and autos were decimated by global competition. In searching for ways to compete, U.S. firms rediscovered and applied Deming's teachings. Since the 1980s, firms such as Motorola, Ford, Kodak, L.L. Bean, and Xerox have become world class practitioners of quality management, with quality levels of just a few defects per million units produced. The suppliers to these firms have also achieved impressively high levels of quality. For example, in 1982 Xerox suppliers were shipping 92 percent defect-free parts. By 1988 these suppliers were shipping 99.97 percent defect-free parts. The measurement and management of quality costs plays an important role in supporting quality management.

▲ THE NATURE OF QUALITY COSTS

Quality is defined as customers' satisfaction with total experience of a product or service. Quality has two dimensions—features and performance. For example, customers may want a personal computer (PC) with sound and video capability (features). If, however, the keyboard locks up or the operating system is not compatible with word processing or spreadsheet software, it is not meeting customer expectations on the performance dimension of quality. This module focuses on the ***performance*** aspect of quality.[1]

In this module, we *define **quality costing*** *as the measurement and management of costs related to providing a customer's required level of product or service performance.* This includes all costs incurred to monitor and prevent problems in product performance, as well as costs incurred to remedy problems that do occur.

The ***objective*** of quality costing is to help management maximize the value customers receive from a product. Failures of product performance create costs for both the firm which produced the product and for its customers. Improving product performance reduces costs for the producing firm because there is less need to spend time reworking defective units, fewer product recalls, and fewer warranty claims. Improved product performance also reduces the cost incurred by customers over the life of the product (referred to as *life-cycle cost,* or *cost of ownership*) by reducing operating, maintenance, and repair costs.

Quality costs have received little attention until fairly recently. Traditional management accounting systems do not separately identify quality costs. Instead, quality costs are subsumed within the costs recorded in many different parts of a firm. For example, the costs associated with spoiled or reworked units may be treated as part of the cost of inventory.[2] Warranty repair costs would be recorded by service departments. Costs of monitoring and preventing quality problems would be recorded by the quality control department.

---

[1] A firm typically meets customer requirements for product features through a target costing system. This subject is discussed in detail in a separate module. The separation of target costing from quality costing is purely a matter of convenience. In practice the line between features and performance is not always clear.

[2] The Modules on Process Costing and Job Order Costing discuss spoilage and rework costs.

In a traditional management accounting system, there is no way to aggregate quality cost items recorded in different departments, so management cannot assess the total quality costs being incurred firm-wide.

Another reason quality costs are not visible in traditional management accounting systems is the combination with other costs. Costs of the quality control department, for instance, are typically part of indirect manufacturing costs (called overhead). However, overhead accounts also record other indirect manufacturing costs such as plant supervisors' salaries, plant payroll processing, and maintenance. The amount recorded as spoilage cost includes not only the costs associated with defective units produced, but also the cost of any units stolen or broken during handling, which are not really quality costs.

When quality costs are not separately identified, it is difficult for a firm to know what it is spending on quality. More importantly, it is not possible to assess the effectiveness of a firm's spending on quality. A firm cannot determine whether its quality spending is focused on the right items, or whether the spending on quality is yielding benefits.

Among those firms that do measure quality costs, many classify total quality costs into the categories of prevention, appraisal, internal failure, and external failure.

Prevention costs are costs incurred *to avoid quality problems from occurring.* An example is the cost of training workers so they do not produce defective units.

Appraisal costs are costs associated with *measuring and monitoring* activities related to quality. An example of appraisal costs is the time spent on inspection of output to determine the number of defective units produced.

Internal failure costs are costs incurred *to remedy defects discovered before the product is delivered to the customer.* The cost of reworking defective units is an example of an internal failure cost.

External failure costs are costs incurred *to remedy defects discovered by the customer.* Warranty repair cost is an example of an external failure cost.

▲ THE QUALITY MANAGEMENT SYSTEM

To manage the four types of quality costs listed above, the relationship of these to the quality management system must be understood. Exhibit 1 shows this relationship. The top part of Exhibit 1 presents the six major activities in managing quality. These relations are depicted by the solid line arrows. The bottom part shows the quality costs commonly incurred at each step of the quality management process. These relations are depicted by the broken line arrows. As Exhibit 1 shows, quality management is a recursive process which begins with understanding customer requirements and ends with customer reaction to the product's delivered quality. The six steps are described in the following pages.

Step 1. Understand Customer Requirements.

The first step in managing quality is to understand customer requirements relating to quality. This requires determining what customers want with respect to performance and how important the various dimensions of performance are to the customers. The PC manufacturer must know the relative importance customers place on multi-media versus ability to run other software, the interval between repairs, and other aspects of reliability and usability. For a tax preparation service, the quality requirements may include freedom from errors in tax returns prepared. For a patient checking into a hospital for elective surgery,

Exhibit 1
Quality Management System and Quality Costs

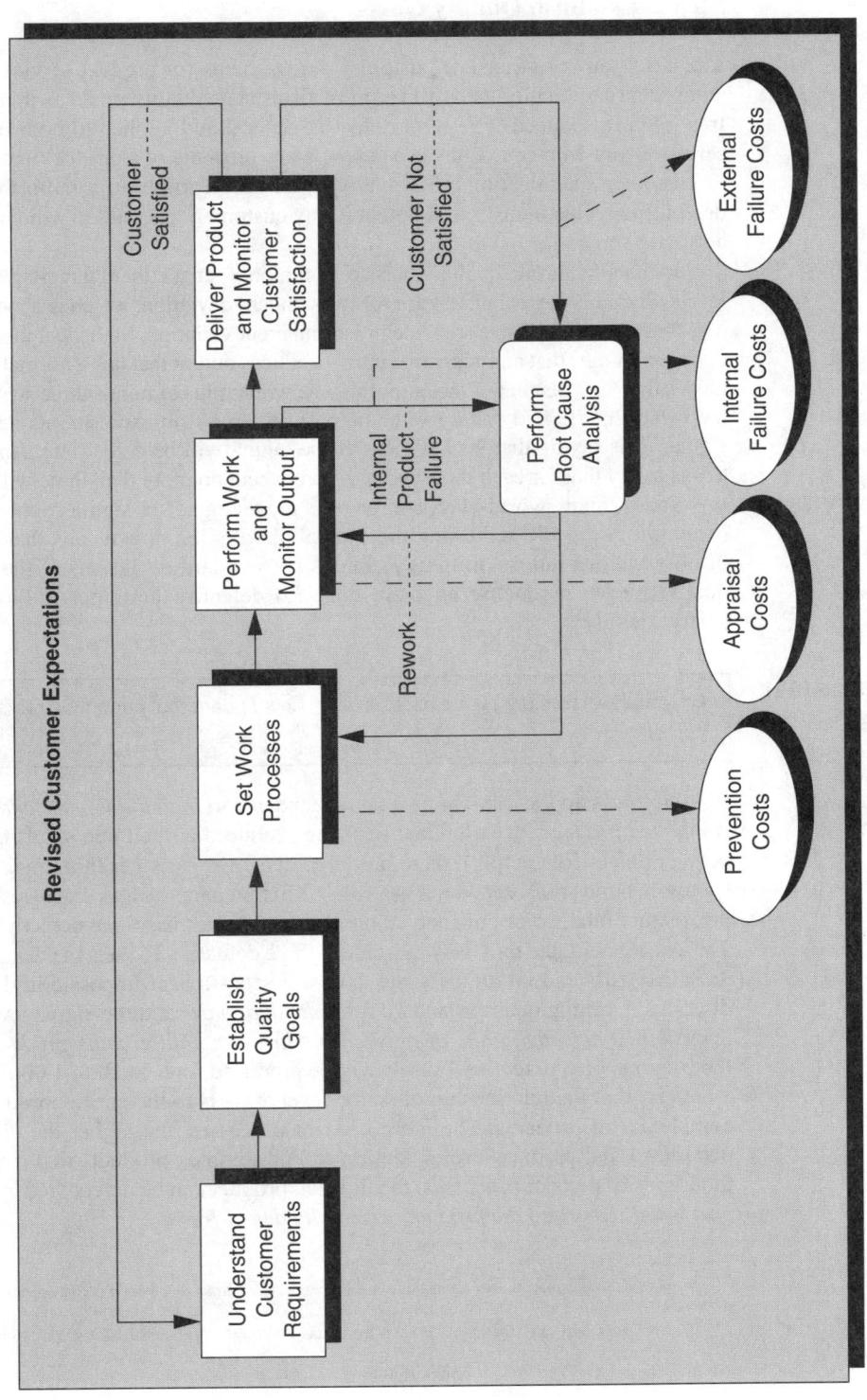

prompt admission and friendly service may be the relevant dimensions of quality. Alaska Airlines seems to understand that customers value the quality of meals and seating comfort.

Step 2. Establish Quality Goals.

The next step is to translate customer requirements for product/service performance into an appropriate quality goal. Today most firms state quality goals as the percent of defect-free output produced. The term defect is general and applies to both manufacturing and service firms. In manufacturing a defect is any attribute of a product that does not conform to customer specifications. For example, an on-off knob on a radio that breaks off is a defect. In service industries, a defect is any customer "encounter" which does not result in a satisfied customer.

In manufacturing, quality goals are commonly set at either "three-sigma" or "six-sigma" levels. Sigma is the technical term for the standard deviation, which is a measure of variation. Most measurements have some degree of inherent variation. Statistical theory used in quality control assumes that a process in control produces output that has a normal distribution.[3] This means that 99.7 percent of the output will be within plus or minus three standard deviations of the mean (the desired value for the output). When a firm expresses its defect rate as "three sigma," it is saying that 99.7 percent of the output will be defect-free. Another way to state this is to say that for each thousand units produced, no more than three will be defective.

Today, many world-class competitors are using a "six-sigma" approach pioneered by Motorola in the 1980s.[4] Using the normal distribution, this means that 99.99966 percent of observations fall within plus or minus six standard deviations of the mean. Six-sigma quality means producing no more than 3.4 defective units per million. This is nearly perfect quality!

Think Along

Do you think six sigma is an excessively high standard that cannot be reached cost-effectively?

Motorola applies six-sigma quality standards to *individual parts and processes, not to completed products.* If individual parts are produced at the three-sigma quality level (99.7 percent defect-free output), there are three defective parts per thousand. Now assume that Motorola builds a TV set which has 1,000 different parts such as chips, resistors, power supply, picture tube, color gun, and so on. Since each part has three defective units, and 1,000 TV sets are built, the only way to produce three defective TV sets in a batch of 1,000 is if all defective parts end up on the same three TV sets—a near impossibility! As Motorola has discovered, setting quality standard for *individual parts* at three-sigma level results in more than *66,810 defective units of finished product per million units produced!* That is, with three sigma, 66.8 defective TV sets will be produced for a batch of 1,000 TV sets.

Note that the relationship of sigma level at parts to the entire product depends on the complexity of products. The more parts or processes, the higher the difference between parts level and product level defect rates. For complex products that require hundreds or thousands of parts or processes, the finished product can be defect-free only if *every single part which goes into the product is virtually defect-free.*

---

[3] A more detailed explanation of sigma limits and properties of a normal distribution is contained in most basic statistics texts.

[4] Ismael Dambolena and Ashok Rao. "What is Six Sigma, Anyway?" *Quality,* Vol. 33, Issue 11, November 1994, p. 10.

Think of an automobile manufacturer with three-sigma quality levels for 10,000 parts or processes. How many defective cars will there be if each part or process uses a three-sigma level? What about an aircraft manufacturer that uses a million parts and processes? How can defect-free output be ensured?

Step 3. Set Work Processes to Meet Quality Goals.

The third step in managing quality is to ensure work processes are designed to produce at the required quality level. This requires adjusting machines, developing control systems, training, and supervising people so quality problems do not occur. Costs incurred on activities undertaken to prevent defects and are called **prevention costs.**

Step 4. Perform Work and Monitor Output.

The next step is to perform work and monitor the output produced to see if quality goals are being met. Quality activities undertaken in this step include inspection of output to detect errors or mistakes. The costs of these activities, which are aimed at making certain that the final output meets the established quality targets, are called **appraisal costs.** When defective units are discovered, any costs incurred for correcting the defectives, which might include rework labor and materials, defect analysis, and error correction are called **internal failure costs.**

Step 5. Deliver Product and Monitor Customer Experience.

The fifth step in the quality management process is to deliver the product and monitor the customer's experience with the product. If the product fails to perform according to customer expectations, the customer may return it for repair or ask for a price adjustment. Any costs related to correcting defects discovered by customers are called **external failure costs.**

If the product does meet customers expectations, the quality management process does not end. Rather, the process begins again with a new assessment of customer expectations for future versions of the product. Most firms have discovered that when customer expectations are met, the customers come to expect even higher levels of performance from future versions of the product. Quality performance becomes a "moving target," and a firm can never become complacent, believing its quality is "good enough."

Step 6. Perform Root Cause Analysis.

The final step in the process is to perform root cause analysis for all internal and external product failures. A root cause analysis determines the underlying cause for product failure. The analysis is designed to find the underlying factors which allowed the problem to occur, and to help the firm identify what corrective measures are needed. A major purpose of the root cause analysis is to determine if certain steps in the process that are causing quality problems should be set at higher tolerance (sigma) levels. The findings of the root cause analysis may be used to redesign work processes to prevent similar problems from recurring.

Measuring and Managing Quality Costs

Exhibit 2
DFP Technologies—Production Process

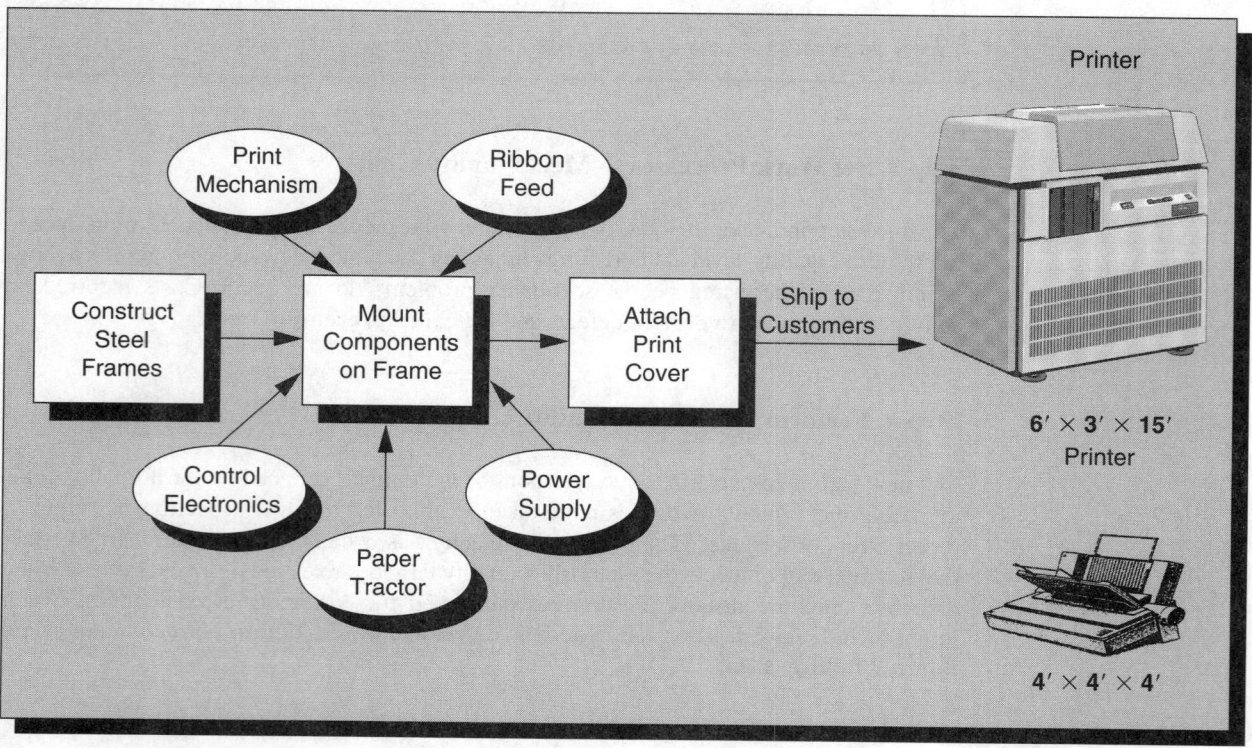

▲ MEASURING QUALITY COSTS—AN ILLUSTRATION

As the flow chart of the quality management system (Exhibit 1) shows, quality costs are incurred at the various stages of the quality management process. To manage quality, measure and report these costs. This section illustrates the measurement of quality costs through the example of a hypothetical firm called **DFP Technologies Inc.** DFP produces large scale printers for high volume applications. Its sales revenue for 1996 is $50,900,000 and its total costs are $45,800,000.

DFP's printers operate at speeds from 1,500 to 6,000 lines per minute. The smallest model is four feet tall and measures approximately four feet by four feet. The largest is six feet tall and measures three feet by 15 feet. DFP's customers are insurance companies, banks, and telephone companies who use the printers for mailings to customers, such as premium notices or bank statements, and other high volume applications such as creating a continuous log of data entry.

The production process used by DFP begins with the construction of steel printer frames. Next, the printer components are mounted on the frame. The components include print mechanisms, control electronics, ribbon feed systems, paper moving mechanisms (tractors), and power supplies. Finally, a printer cover of high grade industrial plastic is attached. The process is depicted in Exhibit 2 above.

Quality is important for DFP's customers, because when a printer is not operating a backlog of work quickly accumulates. In addition to the loss of productive time, recovering from printer downtime involves costs for customers, who may have to pay overtime to data entry operators or hire additional temporary help. Through interaction with customers, DFP has learned that the *two* overriding quality factors most important to its customers are:

1. Minimizing downtime due to printers being out of order.
2. Maintaining high print quality.

DFP's quality goals are set at the three-sigma level for each process step and for each part supplier. This means that both in-house manufacturing and suppliers strive to attain a goal of 99.7 percent defect-free outputs, or producing less than three defective parts per thousand *parts*. Remember that each printer contains several components, including a power supply, paper tractor, control electronics, print mechanism, and ribbon feed. The defect rate for *printers* is substantially higher than three per thousand, because the only way a printer can be defect-free is if *all of the major parts in the printer are defect-free.*

DFP's spending on quality is substantial. However, these costs are not visible because they are buried within the traditional cost categories of materials, wages and salaries, equipment, rent, and utilities. The actual costs for the assembly department, as they would appear in DFP's accounting system, are shown in Exhibit 3 below.

Exhibit 3
DFP Assembly Department—Actual Costs
for Year Ended December 31, 1996

Cost Item	Total Cost
Materials	$8,124,000
Manager's salary	64,000
Supervisors' salaries (3)	102,000
Assembly wages	3,360,000
Equipment	675,000
Rent	270,000
Utilities	90,000
Total	**$12,685,000**

To determine which costs are related to quality, the accountant must interview people in the assembly department and observe work being performed.[5] The results of this analysis are summarized in Exhibit 4.

Think Along

Can you use the information provided in Exhibit 4 to determine what part of the assembly department's spending would be classified as prevention, assessment, internal failure, and external failure costs?

---

[5] This is an application of activity-based management. For a more detailed discussion of that topic see the ABM Module in this series.

Exhibit 4
DFP Assembly Department—Analysis of Actual Costs for Year Ended December 31, 1996

1. **Materials.**
   a. Of the total spending on materials, approximately $194,940 was for spoiled and reworked units.
   b. Of this amount, approximately 40% is for defective units discovered internally.
   c. The remaining 60% is for defects discovered by customers.
2. **Manager's Salary.** The manager spends time in the following activities related to quality.
   a. Fifteen work days attending seminars on preventing quality problems.
   b. Two hours a week analyzing the results of quality inspections.
   c. Ten hours a week searching out causes of problems.
   d. One hour a week meeting with the sales manager to resolve quality problems identified by customers.
3. **Supervisors' Salaries.** There are three supervisors who each spend the following time on quality activities:
   a. 3 hours a week in quality training.
   b. 5 hours a week overseeing rework activities for defects found internally.
   c. 7 hours a week overseeing rework of defects found by customers.
4. **Assembly Wages.** The firm has 120 assembly workers who are paid, on average, $14 per hour. Their quality activities are:
   a. Each employee spends eight hours per year in quality training.
   b. A total of 28,800 hours per year is spent inspecting components purchased from outside suppliers.
   c. A total of 18,000 hours is spent on inspection of printers assembled in the department.
   d. 21 assembly workers spend all of their time reworking defects discovered in the department.
   e. 24 workers spend all of their time reworking defective units returned by customers.
5. **Equipment.** The assembly department's equipment-related expenses were $675,000. This includes the following quality items:
   a. Equipment used in testing—$8,500.
   b. Depreciation on equipment used to correct problems discovered within DFP—$45,000.
   c. Depreciation on equipment used to correct problems discovered by customers—$38,000.
6. **Rent.** The assembly department's share of factory rent is $270,000. Analysis reveals the following:
   a. Approximately 10% of the assembly department space is devoted to inspection.
   b. Approximately 30% of the assembly department space is occupied by area used for rework of defective units. It is estimated that approximately 60% of the units reworked are discovered internally. The rest are problems reported by customers.
7. **Utilities.** Annual utility costs are $90,000. These are assigned to the inspection and rework areas on the basis of the relative amount of space each occupies.

DFP's Assembly Department Quality Costs.

We can use the data in Exhibit 4 to classify DFP's assembly department quality costs into the four categories. The first step in this analysis is to examine each of the eight items in that exhibit and decide whether they are prevention, appraisal, internal, or external failure costs. For example, materials used for spoiled and defective units (Item 1, Exhibit 4) are failure costs. These are internal failure costs if the defective units are discovered before shipment, otherwise these are external failure costs. Similarly, the cost of the manager's time attending quality seminars (Item 2a, Exhibit 4) is a prevention cost. The other items can be similarly classified. The results are shown in Exhibit 5.

Exhibit 5
Four-Way Classification of Assembly Department Costs

	Quality Cost Element	Classification
1.	**Materials.**	
	a. Internal defects	Internal failure
	b. Customer discovered defects	External failure
2.	**Manager's Salary.**	
	a. Attending seminars on preventing quality problems	Prevention
	b. Analyzing the results of quality inspections	Appraisal
	c. Searching out causes of problems	Internal failure
	d. Resolving quality problems identified by customers	External failure
3.	**Supervisors' Salaries.**	
	a. Quality training	Prevention
	b. Overseeing rework of defects found internally	Internal failure
	c. Rework of defects found by customers	External failure
4.	**Assembly Workers.**	
	a. Quality training	Prevention
	b. Inspecting components purchased from suppliers	Appraisal
	c. Inspection of the printers assembled by DFP	Appraisal
	d. Reworking defects discovered in the department	Internal failure
	e. Reworking defective units returned by customers	External failure
5.	**Equipment.**	
	a. Equipment used in testing	Appraisal
	b. Depreciation—problems discovered within DFP	Internal failure
	c. Depreciation—problems discovered by customers	External failure
6.	**Rent.**	
	a. Factory space devoted to inspection	Appraisal
	b. Factory space for rework of defective units—60% internally; 40% customers	Internal failure (60%)
		External failure (40%)
7.	**Utilities.**	
	a. Factory space devoted to inspection	Appraisal
	b. Factory space for rework of defective units—60% internally; 40% customers	Internal failure (60%)
		External failure (40%)

The next step is to rearrange the items in Exhibit 5 into the four categories of prevention, appraisal, internal failure, and external failure costs. Also, the costs shown in Exhibit 3 must be assigned to each of the cost items. This provides the view of DFP's assembly department's quality costs presented in Exhibit 6.

Exhibit 6
Quality Costs—Assembly Department

Ex. 2 Ref.	Cost Element	Calculation	Amount
	Prevention Costs		
2 a	Manager's Salary—attending seminars	([15 × 8) ÷ 2000]) × 64,000	$3,840
3 a	Supervisors' Salaries—quality training	([3 × 50 × 3] ÷ 6,000[1]) × 102,000	7,650
4 a	Assembly Workers—quality training	8 × 120 × $14	13,440
	Total Prevention Costs		**$24,930**
	Appraisal Costs		
2 b	Manager's Salary—analyzing results	2 ÷ 40 × 64,000	$3,200
	Assembly Wages—		
4 b	Inspection of outside components	28,800 × $14	403,200
4 c	Inspection of printers assembled	18,000 × $14	252,000
5 a	Equipment—used in testing		8,500
6 a	Rent—inspection space	.10 × 270,000	27,000
7 a	Utilities—inspection space	.10 × 90,000	9,000
	Total Appraisal Costs		**$702,900**
	Internal Failure Costs		
1 a	Materials—internal defects	.40 × 194,940	$77,976
2 c	Manager's Salary—searching causes	10 ÷ 40 × 64,000	16,000
3 b	Supervisors' Salaries—overseeing rework	([3 × 50 × 3]/6,000) × 102,000	12,750
4 d	Assembly Wages—reworking defects	21 × 2,000 × 14	588,000
5 b	Equipment—internal problems		45,000
6 b	Rent—rework area	.30 × 270,000 × .60	48,600
7 b	Utilities—rework area	.30 × 90,000 × .60	16,200
	Total Internal Failure Costs		**$804,526**
	External Failure Costs		
1 a	Materials—external defects	.60 × 194,940	$116,964
2 d	Manager's Salary—sales meeting	.1 ÷ 40 × 64,000	1,600
3 c	Supervisors' Salaries—reworking defects	([7 × 50 × 3] ÷ 6,000) × 102,000	17,850
4 e	Assembly Wages—reworking defects	24 × 2,000 × 14	672,000
5 c	Equipment—external problems		38,000
6 b	Rent—rework area	.30 × 270,000 × .40	32,400
7 b	Utilities—rework area	.30 × 90,000 × .40	10,800
	Total External Failure Costs		**$889,614**
	Total Quality Costs		**$2,421,970**

[1] Assumes each of 3 supervisors works 40 hours per week 50 weeks a year, so 3 × 40 × 50 = 6000 hours.

The quality cost analysis for the assembly department at DFP Technologies would generate the quality cost report shown in Exhibit 7.

Exhibit 7
DFP's Assembly Department—Quality Cost Report for the Year Ended December 31, 1996

Cost Item	Prevention	Appraisal	Internal Failure	External Failure	Total Quality Cost	Total Department Cost
Materials			$77,976	$116,964	$194,940	$8,124,000
Manager's salary	3,840	3,200	16,000	1,600	24,640	64,000
Supervisors' salaries	7,650		12,750	17,850	38,250	102,000
Assembly wages	13,440	403,200	588,000	672,000	1,928,640	3,360,000
		252,000				
Equipment		8,500	45,000	38,000	91,500	675,000
Rent		27,000	48,600	32,400	108,000	270,000
Utilities		9,000	16,200	10,800	36,000	90,000
Totals	**$24,930**	**$702,900**	**$804,526**	**$889,614**	**$2,421,970**	**$12,685,000**

Key Point — The quality cost analysis demonstrates the kaleidoscopic nature of cost analysis in today's complex organizations. Costs can be viewed from different perspectives, just as each turn of a kaleidoscope presents a unique pattern. The traditional cost data (Exhibit 3) is one view, while the quality cost report (Exhibit 7) presents a different view.

While the information in this exhibit provides the necessary detail for the cost analysis, the accountant will need to organize the information differently to report to management. The report shown in Exhibit 7 accomplishes this.

Firm-Wide Analysis of Quality Costs.

In order to understand the full impact of quality costs, the accountants at DFP must perform an analysis similar to that shown for the assembly department in each department of the firm. Assume this is done and the firm-wide quality cost report is as shown in Exhibit 8.

Exhibit 8
DFP Technologies—Quality Cost Report for the Year Ended December 31, 1996

	Engineering	Purchasing	Assembly	Other Depts.	Totals	% of Total QC
Prevention	$505,900	$8,400	$ 24,930	$ 248,520	$ 787,750	13
Appraisal	46,000	40,600	702,900	184,700	974,200	16
Internal failure	320,800	260,200	804,526	841,124	2,226,650	38
External failure	476,500	295,400	889,614	299,886	1,961,400	33
Total	$1,349,200	$604,600	$2,421,970	$1,574,230	**$5,950,000**	100

Think Along — Based on the information presented in firm-wide quality cost report, what conclusions can you draw about how DFP is managing their spending on quality?

MMQC–13

▲ USING QUALITY COST DATA TO MANAGE QUALITY

The quality cost information can help DFP's management address five important quality management issues:

- ▲ What is the total *amount* of spending on quality management throughout the firm? How is this amount *distributed* across different areas of the firm?
- ▲ What is the relative amount the firm is spending within each *cost category*?
- ▲ Is the spending on quality producing tangible *financial benefits* to the firm?
- ▲ Is the spending on quality *focused on customer satisfaction*?
- ▲ What are the *root causes* of quality problems and how much is being spent on eliminating them?

Firm-Wide Spending on Quality.

To manage quality costs, management must know how much it is spending on quality activities in total, and where in the firm quality costs are being incurred. The firm-wide quality cost report (Exhibit 8) shows that DFP's total quality costs are $5,950,000. This represents approximately 11.7 percent of DFP's total sales of $50,900,000 (5,950,000 ÷ 50,900,000 = .1168).

Clearly, quality costs have a substantial impact on DFP's profitability. In many industries, average firm profits are less than 10 percent of sales revenue. If this is true for DFP, eliminating quality costs *would double firm profit*.

Without the quality cost information, DFP would not have been able to evaluate the firm-wide effect of quality. Individual departments measure quality in a variety of ways. For example, engineering typically measures quality by the number of design changes. Purchasing would measure quality as billing errors. Accounts receivable might measure quality as the number of errors in customer accounts. These measurements provide useful information, but there is no way to combine them. It is meaningless to add design changes to billing errors to misstatements of customer accounts. Combination can be accomplished only when these measures are translated into dollar terms, and the total effect on the company made visible.

Another important insight from the firm-wide quality cost report is that quality costs are incurred throughout the firm. Many firms have the notion that "quality is manufacturing's job," and quality costs are incurred only in production and assembly departments. As the DFP example demonstrates, however, the assembly department is not the only area of the firm with substantial quality costs. In fact, the quality costs in assembly are only about 41 percent of the firm's total quality costs (2,421,970 ÷ 5,950,000 = .407).

Spending on Quality by Categories.

In order to manage quality effectively, the firm needs to evaluate whether spending is focused on the right quality activities. Firm-wide, DFP's spending on prevention is just 13 percent of total quality costs, and appraisal is 16 percent. Combined, prevention and appraisal are less than internal failure costs, which are 38 percent of total quality costs. In addition, the large amount of external failure costs is of particular concern because these costs represent quality problems which impact customers.

Large as it is, the measure of external failure costs underestimates the cost DFP bears because of quality problems experienced by customers. A more complete estimate would include such intangible items as lost goodwill and diminished reputation. The loss of future sales revenue is also relevant. For example, DFP might learn through sales representatives that a dissatisfied customer is planning to replace his equipment with a printer from a different vendor. The lost profit from that customer would be an external failure cost for DFP. Research has found that for consumer products, on average, every dissatisfied customer tells 19 others, and those individuals' purchasing decisions may be affected as well. Although the financial impact of lost sales is not a cost item recorded in traditional management accounting systems, it is in a very real sense a quality cost.

Another insight from DFP's firm-wide quality cost report (Exhibit 8) is that a relatively large amount is being spent on appraisal compared to prevention. You will recall that appraisal costs represent inspection and monitoring costs. The high appraisal cost suggests that DFP is relying on inspections to correct defects rather than investing in prevention activities to ensure that defective units are not produced. Inspecting quality in after-the-fact is generally more costly and is less effective in the long-run than redesigning work processes to ensure that defective output is not produced in the first place.

Financial Returns from Quality Costs.

An effective quality management program can provide a positive financial return by improving quality, reducing cost, and speeding time to market. Many firms have specific financial goals for quality programs. For example, AT&T requires all quality programs to produce at least a 10 percent financial return. One way to measure the financial impact of quality programs is to look at what happens to the categories of quality costs over time. Research shows that firms without quality costing systems frequently have quality costs between 15 and 20 percent of revenues. Firms with effective quality cost measurement systems, in contrast, normally have quality costs less than five percent of revenue. This exhibit suggests that one important financial return from the measurement of quality costs is reduction in the level of quality costs.

Key Point

The experience of many firms who have invested in quality shows that improving product quality actually reduces the total spending on quality.

Think Along

How can improving product/service quality reduce a firm's total spending on quality?

There are two main reasons for this. First, as more is spent on prevention and appraisal to improve quality, there is a corresponding reduction in failure costs. Failure costs are much greater in magnitude than prevention and appraisal costs, however. The increased spending on prevention and appraisal needed to improve quality is more than offset by reduced failure costs, with the result that total quality costs decrease.

Consider what might happen if DFP increases spending for prevention and appraisal by 20 percent. This would require a cash outlay of $352,390 (787,750 + 974,200 = 1,761,950 × .2 = 352,390). If this spending achieves a 20 percent reduction in failure costs, this will generate savings of $837,610 (2,226,650 + 1,961,400 = 4,188,050 × .2 =

Exhibit 9
Relationship of Quality Costs to Defect Level[6]

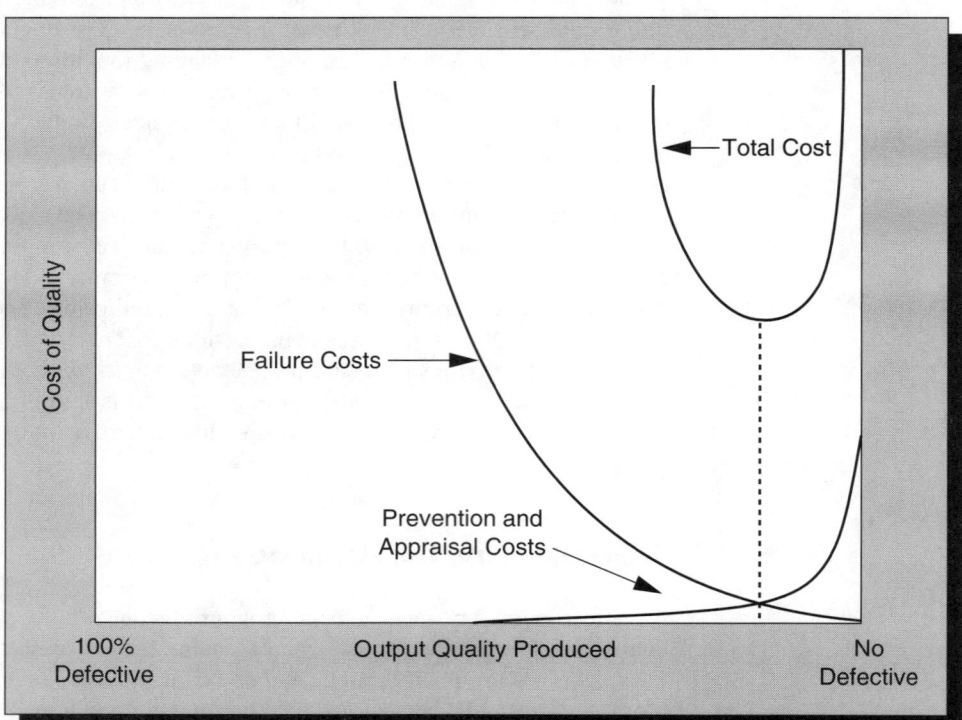

837,610). The combined effect is a reduction in total quality costs of $485,220 (837,610 failure cost savings − 352,390 increased prevention/appraisal costs).

The quality tradeoff function shown in Exhibit 9 depicts this relationship between spending on prevention/appraisal, failure costs, and the level of total quality costs.

As Exhibit 9 shows, a firm which produces poor quality output is probably spending little on prevention and appraisal, and will incur high failure costs. Conversely, a firm producing close to zero defects may be spending more on prevention and appraisal, but lower failure costs will likely result in lower total quality costs. As the firm moves toward zero defects, this tradeoff between higher spending on prevention/appraisal and lower failure costs results in a total quality cost curve which is U-shaped. The lowest point on the curve, which represents the minimum total quality costs, is very close to the zero defect end of the scale.

The other way in which improved quality reduces total quality costs is through long term reduction in overall spending for prevention and appraisal activities. As quality becomes a routine part of the production process, firms frequently find there is less need for monitoring and inspecting (appraisal costs) or to redesign products/processes (prevention costs).

For strategic decision making, a firm needs a way to estimate potential cost savings from improved quality management. Remember that quality goals are commonly expressed as sigma levels, which refer to the probability of producing a defective part.

---

[6] This chart has been adapted from J. M. Juran, Leonard A. Seder, and Frank M. Gryna, Jr. editors. *Quality Control Handbook,* New York; McGraw-Hill, 1962.

The financial impact of improved quality on total quality costs can be illustrated by considering what would happen if DFP were to move from its current level of quality performance (three sigma) to the world class level of six sigma. Currently, the company is spending a total of $4,188,050 on failure costs ($2,226,650 in internal failure costs plus $1,961,400 in external failure costs). This amount represents 8.2 percent of its sales revenue (4,188,050 ÷ 50,900,000 = 0.082). This spending level is for three-sigma quality which yields approximately eight defective printers per 100 produced.

Motorola and other firms operating at "six-sigma"[7] quality levels have found failure costs commonly less than one percent of sales revenue. If DFP were to adopt a six-sigma strategy and to experience similar savings, its failure costs could be reduced to one percent of sales, or $509,000 (.01 × 50,900,000). This would provide failure cost savings of $3,679,050 (4,188,050 − 509,000).

If DFP needed to double spending on prevention and appraisal to achieve six-sigma quality levels, this would cost an additional $1,761,950 (787,750 + 974,200). Overall, the total quality costs would still be reduced by $1,917,100 (failure cost savings of $3,679,050 minus increased prevention/appraisal of $1,761,950). This amount would represent a savings of approximately 3.8 percent of sales revenue (1,917,950 ÷ 50,900,000 = .0377). Over time, as the six-sigma quality performance becomes a way of life in the organization, the firm may be able to reduce spending on prevention and appraisal, generating additional financial benefit.

Exhibit 10 shows the impact of improving quality on total quality costs. Cost is measured as a percent of sales revenue and quality is measured in terms of sigma level (defect rates) produced. Typical firm experience shows that as quality improves from four sigma levels to six sigma, quality costs decline from 10 percent of sales to two or three percent of total sales.

Think Along

> How can DFP use its analysis of quality costs to meet its strategic objective of satisfying customers' expectations regarding product performance?

Quality Spending and Customer Satisfaction.

The ultimate test of any quality management program is how well it helps the firm meet customer expectations. DFP can use its quality cost data to determine how well the pattern of its spending on quality matches the relative importance placed on each dimension by its customers. This is accomplished by constructing a *Value Index*. A Value Index is the ratio of a customer's perceived importance of a performance dimension to a firm's spending on that dimension.

When the Value Index is greater than one, *the importance of that performance dimension to customers is relatively larger than the firm's quality spending for that dimension*. This suggests the firm may want to consider increasing quality spending for that dimension. When the Value Index is less than one, *the importance of that dimension to customers is relatively lower than the firm's quality spending for that dimension*. This suggests the firm should consider whether it may be spending too much money on that dimension.

---

[7] Motorola embarked on a six-sigma quality program in the early 1980s which improved its quality tenfold, reduced manufacturing costs, and decreased time to market for its products.

Exhibit 10
Impact of Improving Quality on Quality Costs

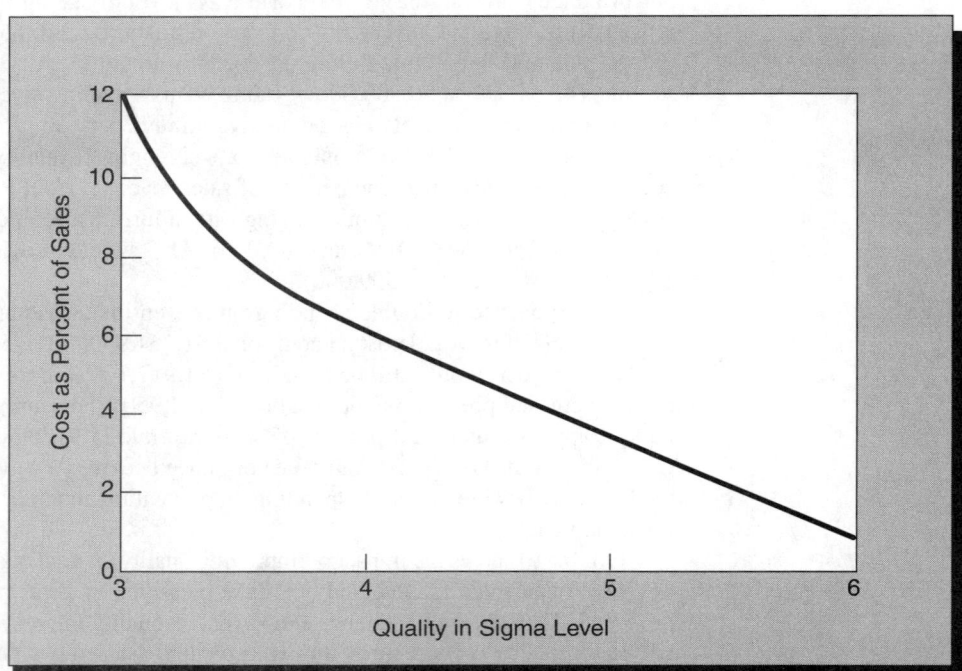

Constructing the Value Index requires a firm to complete three steps. These steps are developing a customer ranking of performance dimensions, estimating quality costs related to each performance dimension, and computing the Value Index.

Step 1. Develop customer ranking of performance dimensions.

The analysis begins with identifying the dimensions of printer performance, as defined by the customer. How important a given dimension of printer performance is to customers depends on *the costs the customer incurs* each time the problem occurs. This may be quite different from the costs incurred by the firm for that dimension of product performance. The analysis of DFP's quality costs thus far has considered only the quality costs incurred by DFP. To complete the analysis, and provide the strategic link to satisfying customer expectations, DFP will need to consider quality costs incurred by its customers.

From the customer's perspective, the quality costs associated with a specific dimension of printer performance would include costs associated with downtime while the printer is being repaired and any maintenance or service fees paid to DFP for printer repair. Assume that based on conversations and customer surveys, DFP has determined that the two quality dimensions most important to customers are downtime and print quality.

One way DFP might estimate its customers' quality costs related to the dimensions of printer performance would be to conduct a detailed activity analysis jointly with the customer. This would involve identifying the activities the customer performs whenever a given dimension of printer performance fails. For example, attempting to restore lost files or re-keying lost data entry work might be required whenever the printer goes down. Estimation of the time required for such activities can be combined with appropriate wage and salary information to provide estimates of the customer's quality costs.

The activity analysis of customer quality costs can be very time consuming and requires close cooperation, as well as considerable trust, between the firm and its customers. A simpler approach can be used to develop rough rule-of-thumb guidelines to estimate customer costs. The customer's personnel can be asked to assign 100 "importance points" to the dimensions of printer performance, based on relative importance. A dimension considered more important will be assigned more points. If DFP finds that its customers consider downtime four times as important as print quality, the customer performance ranking would appear as shown in Exhibit 11.

Exhibit 11
Customer's Importance Ranking of Printer Performance

Dimensions of Printer Performance	Importance Ranking
Downtime	80%
Print quality	20%

Step 2. Estimate quality costs related to each performance dimension.

The next step in the analysis is for DFP to determine what proportion of its quality cost relates to each of these two dimensions of printer performance. Assume DFP's service logs show the three causes of printer downtime are faulty ribbon motion, improper paper feed, and overheating. Similarly, assume that print quality problems result from broken print hammers or paper feed misalignment. DFP must now determine how its spending on quality relates to the five causal factors of ribbon motion faults, paper feed problems, overheating, broken print hammers, and paper feed misalignment.

Exhibit 12
Quality Costs by Customer Performance Requirements

Customer Defined Performance Dimension	Prevention	Assessment	Internal Failure	External Failure	Total
Customer downtime					
Ribbon motion fault	$55,200	$225,600	$583,680	$487,435	$1,351,915
Paper feed problems	343,931	685,380	665,400	716,145	2,410,856
Overheating	34,548	95,800	153,760	69,700	353,808
Subtotal					4,116,579
Print quality					
Broken print hammers	217,451	339,365	461,763	253,664	1,272,243
Paper feed misalignment	86,620	78,055	162,047	234,456	561,178
Subtotal					1,833,421
Total	$737,750	$1,424,200	$2,026,650	$1,761,400	$5,950,000

DFP can assign its total quality costs of $5,950,000 to these five causes by using an activity analysis similar to that used to develop the quality cost reports shown in Exhibits 7 and 8. DFP will have to analyze all activities and resources related to preventing, monitoring, and reworking problems related to these five causes. Assume this analysis has been done, and the result is the report shown in Exhibit 12. DFP can now see that, of its total quality spending of $5,950,000, 69 percent relates to printer downtime (4,116,579 ÷ 5,950,000 = .69). The remaining 31 percent of DFP's quality costs relate to the performance dimension of print quality (1,833,421 ÷ 5,950,000 = .308).

Step 3. Compute the Value Index.

The customer value data (Exhibit 11) can now be combined with DFP's cost data (Exhibit 12), to construct the Value Index for the two customer-defined performance dimensions of printer downtime and print quality. Exhibit 13, below, shows the calculation of the Value Index.

Exhibit 13
Value Index for DFP's Printer Performance Dimensions

Dimensions of Printer Performance	Importance Ranking	Quality Cost	Value Index (Col. 2 ÷ 3)	Action Needed
Downtime or shut-down time	80%	69%	1.16	Requires more attention/cost
Print quality and legibility	20%	31%	0.645	Requires less attention/cost

Think Along

Based on the Value Index, how would you suggest DFP adjust its spending on quality to improve customer satisfaction?

DFP appears to be spending too little on the performance dimension of printer downtime. While 69 percent of DFP's quality spending relates to this dimension, customers assigned it a value rating of 80 percent. Notice that this performance dimension has a Value Index greater than 1.00. This indicates that the firm is underspending on this performance dimension. In contrast, 31 percent of DFP's quality spending relates to print quality, which received an importance rating of only 20 percent from the customers. As a general rule, a firm can improve the effectiveness of its quality management by increasing spending on performance dimensions with a Value Index greater than one. This rule does not apply to items which have very low importance rankings or very low quality costs, however.

The Value Index is a powerful strategic tool because it focuses attention on customer requirements. It shows a firm how to allocate its spending on quality in order to provide the greatest value to customers. DFP now knows that it must find ways to address the causes that result in printer downtime for its customers.

Root Cause Analysis of Quality.

To eliminate downtime or improve print quality, we must address the causes behind these problems. A *root cause analysis* is a systematic method of linking a problem, as perceived by the customer, to the underlying causes in order to identify the appropriate corrective action. Exhibit 14 provides an abbreviated root cause analysis for DFP's printer problems.

As Exhibit 14 shows, downtime may result from one of three *first level causes*. These are ribbon motion failure, paper misfeed, and overheating. Ribbon motion failure, in turn, is caused by failure of either the sensors or the circuit board. These are the *second level causes*. For conciseness, the root cause analysis shown in Exhibit 14 shows only these two levels of analysis. To determine how to remedy the problem of printer downtime, however, DFP would need to carry the analysis further. For example, DFP may determine that circuit board failure is caused by either a defective chip or faulty resistor. The chip, in turn, may

Exhibit 14
A Partial Root Cause Analysis for DFP Printers

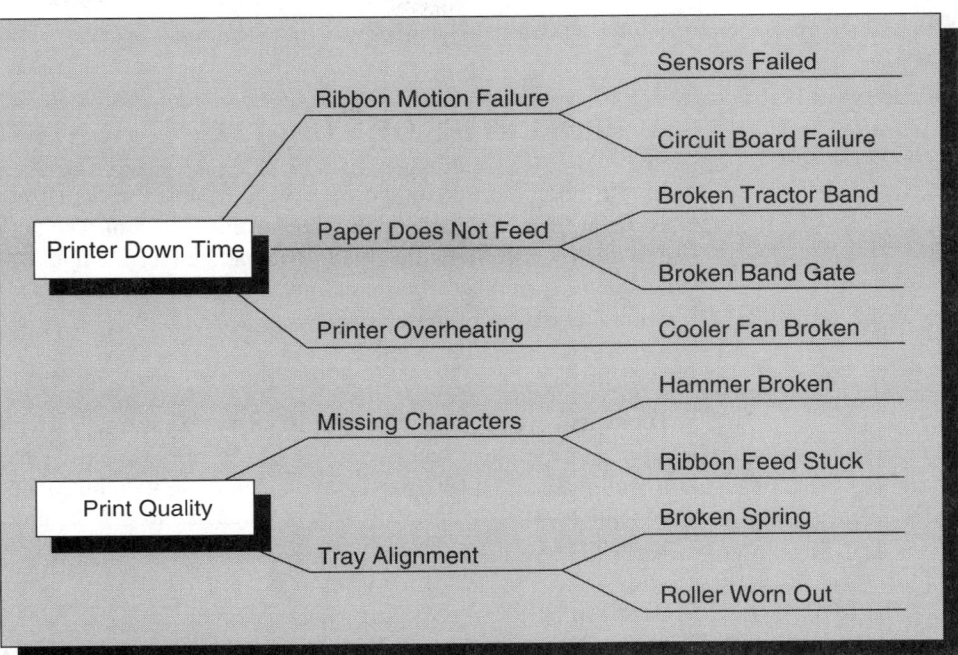

have failed because of improper specifications. When the analysis is carried through to ultimate causes in this way, DFP can see that to reduce printer downtime resulting from ribbon motion faults it must redesign the chip to correct specifications.

Most firms find it takes four or five levels of analysis to identify root causes. For this reason, Toyota, and other firms that use root cause analysis refer to this approach as the *"five why's."* The idea is that root causes can only be found by asking "why" several times to understand the multiple levels of causes of performance failures. Because of the appearance of the root cause diagram, these are often referred to as *fishbone diagrams*.

Quality cost data can be used with root cause analysis to focus quality spending on elimination of the more costly causes of product failure. DFP can assess the appropriateness of its quality spending related to ribbon motion faults by examining costs in each category (prevention, appraisal, internal, and external failure) for each of the causes of ribbon motion faults (sensor failure, faulty circuit board). For example, DFP might find that, of the $1,071,115 in failure costs for ribbon motion faults, 80 percent relates to sensor failures. The analysis might also find that sensor failures account for only 40 percent of the prevention and appraisal costs of ribbon motion faults. In that case, DFP should increase spending on prevention and appraisal related to sensor failure and monitor failure costs associated with this cause to see if it declines.

The combination of root cause analysis and quality cost data for each root cause can be a powerful tool to help management prioritize quality spending. An important contribution of root cause analysis is that it helps management to see the relative contribution of each cause to failure costs. Organizations that perform this type of analysis discover that a relatively small number of causes are responsible for most of the failure costs. A rule of thumb used by industry is the "80–20 rule." This rule asserts that root causes have a *Pareto distribution* so that 20 percent of the root causes are responsible for 80 percent of the failure costs. By helping to identify *which root causes* are the 20 percent that cause 80 percent of costs, quality cost analysis can help management focus quality improvement efforts to achieve maximum benefit.

▲ PROPERTIES OF A QUALITY COST SYSTEM

As the prior discussion shows, a well-designed system for measuring quality costs is essential for an effective quality management system. The properties that must be present in a quality cost system if it is to be an effective strategic tool will be addressed next. In designing quality cost systems, managers must consider the technical, behavioral, and cultural attributes of these systems.

Technical Attributes of a Quality Cost System.

A well-designed quality cost system should provide information relevant to management decision making and provide a better understanding of the process that leads these costs to be incurred.

Decision relevance.
The analysis of quality costs provides information relevant to many managerial decisions related to quality. In the previous section several key decisions that require quality cost data were discussed. For instance, to make informed decisions about quality, management needs to know how much it is spending on quality, where in the firm the spending occurs, what is the purpose of the spending, and how quality impacts the firm's profitability. This information can help management balance cost and quality considerations intelligently and to focus its spending on eliminating the critical root causes that account for quality problems, resulting in improved customer satisfaction and lower total quality costs.

Process understanding.
A well-designed system for measuring quality costs can help managers understand what causes, or drives, quality costs to be incurred. Tracing quality costs to the root causes, as shown in Exhibit 14, requires a horizontal flow of information across departments. This is because root causes often are the result of decisions made in other departments than where the costs are incurred, and also because a single decision may result in quality costs being incurred in several departments. The only way to understand the firm-wide impact of each root cause is through this type of horizontal analysis. This in turn helps management understand interdependencies between departments. Process understanding can be further enhanced by extending the analysis to include other value chain members such as suppliers and customers. The focus on the entire value chain helps to make visible how the design of work relationships lead to quality problems or improvements.

Behavioral Attributes of a Quality Cost System.

A well-designed quality costing system must lead to behaviors that support an organization's strategic goals of quality, cost, and time. Three positive behavioral consequences of measuring and reporting quality costs are: (1) greater responsiveness to customer requirements; (2) improved attitudes and aspirations about quality, and (3) better management of quality costs through visibility. A possible dysfunctional behavioral consequence is creating an incentive to pad budgets.

Focus on customer requirements.

By computing the cost and value of particular performance characteristics of a product, a quality cost system can link actions and decisions to customer requirements. This information helps people understand how their daily activities impact the product's performance in the hands of a customer and what value the customer places on these performance dimensions. The people in DFP who manufacture or assemble the paper feed can see how important it is to a customer and how much it costs DFP in failure costs when the paper feed fails. This helps them to see the importance of their actions in satisfying customer expectations. When workers see that reducing quality costs not only frees up resources, but leads to a higher level of customer satisfaction, there is a subtle but important shift in attitude. The negative focus on attacking defects as problems can be replaced with the more positive attitude of striving to exceed customer expectations.

Improved attitudes and aspirations about quality.

Traditional accounting systems focus on classifying and recording the cost of spoiled units as normal or abnormal spoilage. This approach assumes that a certain level of defects and waste is expected. The unfortunate behavioral impact of this approach is that there is no motivation to reduce defects or spoilage classified as "normal" by the accounting system. Also, when the only quality costs recognized are in production departments, there is no aspiration for the (potentially much greater) quality improvements which can come from product redesign. Measuring quality costs is a way to encourage people to reduce these costs and not just accept them.

Better management through visibility.

The type of firm-wide analysis of quality costs conducted by DFP Technologies can serve as an important awareness tool, informing decision makers of the impact of quality on the company's financial performance. Until quality measures are translated into financial terms, there cannot be aggregation across the entire firm. When quality costs are measured and become visible, people focus attention on those activities which have a favorable impact on quality costs.

Another element of visibility is the use of the term failure costs. The language conveys a subtle but important message that certain actions cause failures. No one likes to admit that their actions result in failure. This language can be an effective way to send a clear message that these costs are undesirable and should be avoided.

Budget padding.

The four-way classification of quality costs can have one potential dysfunctional behavioral impact in the short run—budget padding. Reductions in failure costs are not seen until well into the future, while prevention costs have to be incurred today. There is a danger that future reductions in failure costs can become a "holy grail" used to justify any budget increase. Management must make certain that quality spending does not become a way to "pad" departmental budgets by allowing these categories to build budgetary slack.

Cultural Attributes of a Quality Cost System.

A good quality cost measurement system can create an organizational culture in which quality becomes a way of life and a central ethical value.

Quality as a way of life.
Accounting, as the language of business, has the ability to frame the terms in which to think about and discuss issues. It has the aura of rationality that lends credence and respectability to issues that may have not been previously considered. A quality cost system has the potential for creating a value system in which quality becomes a way of life in the organization. By measuring quality and putting customers at the center of quality cost management, a customer-focused value system can be created. These values, once internalized, can provide an organization with a healthy organizational culture in the long run.

Quality as an ethical value.
Quality can be an important ethical issue in cases where product failures are life threatening, as in the tragic Challenger disaster, when the failure of a small component called O-ring resulted in the loss of the astronauts' lives. In these situations, financial measures of external failure costs may be inadequate. Further, the implication that a given level of defects is normal and to be expected is unacceptable.

The story of the Model 700 rifle manufactured by Remington Arms Co. illustrates the serious ethical considerations which can be related to product quality. In 1994 a jury awarded $17 million in damages to a man whose foot had to be amputated when he was injured by a Remington Model 700 which fired accidentally.[8] Evidence indicated that the company had known as early as 1979 that the model could easily fire without the trigger being pulled. The company had estimated the cost to fix the defective trigger mechanism to be 32 cents per gun. The company decided against a product recall, however, indicating that only one percent of the rifles were estimated to be defective, which meant two million rifles would have to be recalled to discover just 20,000 defects.

For some products, a one percent defect rate might be considered adequate. For the customer who lost his foot, however, this is entirely unacceptable. The total cost to Remington of this quality failure goes well beyond the millions of dollars in judgments in this and other pending lawsuits. The loss of public trust and damage to the firm's reputation will continue to plague the firm for years to come.

▲ LESSONS LEARNED

There are several important lessons to learn from this module.

- ▲ Traditional management accounting systems do not separately identify quality costs. Because these costs are not measured and reported, management may not realize how large these costs are and how important it is to manage them.
- ▲ Quality costs are part of a firm's quality management system. Quality management requires understanding customer requirements for performance and translating these requirements into appropriate quality goals for work processes.

---

[8] See Loren Berger. "Remington Faces a Misfiring Squad," Business Week, May 23, 1994, p. 90.

▲ There are four types of quality costs, including prevention and appraisal costs, which are incurred to prevent or measure product failures, and internal and external failure costs, which result from product failures either within the plant or after delivery to customers.

▲ Quality costs help quality management by informing management about the amount spent on quality, the distribution of quality spending throughout the firm, the financial benefits from improved quality, the extent to which quality spending is aligned with customer requirements, and the amount spent on preventing particular root causes of failure.

▲ A well-designed quality cost system must support quality management decisions, provide an understanding of how the design of work processes results in quality costs, encourage behaviors that enhance quality, and create a culture in which customer expectations are not just met but exceeded.

▲ COMMON TERMS

Activity The series of related tasks that are part of work performed in an organization. It represents what is done such as the several things needed to load a truck with goods to be shipped, or responding to a customer complaint. (See process diagram.)

Activity Based Costing (ABC) A method of costing in which activities are the primary cost objects. ABC measures cost and performance of activities, and assigns the costs of those activities to other cost objects, such as products or customers, based on their use of activities.

Allocation The apportionment or distribution of a common cost between two or more cost objects. In accounting, allocation is usually a way of assigning a cost between cost objects (products, departments or processes) that share that common cost. An allocation involves dividing the cost needed to allocate by some physical quantity (ideally a cost driver).

Benchmarking The process of investigating and identifying "best practices" and using them as a standard to improve one's own processes and activities.

Budget A quantitative plan of action that helps an organization coordinate resource inflows and outflows for a specific time period. Budgets are usually financial but may also include nonfinancial operating information.

Capacity The physical facilities, personnel, supplier contacts, and processes necessary to meet the product or service needs of customers.

Cost A monetary measure of the resources consumed by a product, service, function, or activity. It also refers to the price paid for acquiring a product or service.

Cost Driver An event or factor that has a systematic relationship to a particular type of cost and causes that cost to be incurred.

Cost Management The systematic analysis of cost drivers for the purpose of understanding how to reduce or maintain costs.

Cost Object Any item (activity, customer, project, work unit, product, channel, or service) for which a measurement of cost is desired.

Competitive Analysis Tools that enable companies to quantify how performance and costs compare against competitors, understand why performance and costs are different, and apply that insight to strengthen competitive responses and implement proactive plans.

Continuous Improvement A program to improve the strategic variables of quality, cost or time in small incremental steps on a continuous basis.

Culture The collective values, beliefs, ethics, and mindsets of the members of an organization, clan, or society which is subconsciously used to interpret events and take action. It is often called the collective programming of the subconscious mind.

Extended Enterprise The extended enterprise includes an organization's customers, suppliers, dealers, and recyclers. It captures the interdependencies across these separate organizations. It is also referred to as the value chain.

Fixed Cost A cost element that does not vary with changes in production volume in the short-run. The property taxes on a factory building is an example of a fixed production cost.

Incremental Cost 1. The cost associated with increasing the output of an activity or project above some base level. 2. The additional cost associated with selecting one economic or business alternative over another, such as difference between working overtime or subcontracting the work.

Indirect Costs   Costs that are not directly assignable or traceable to a cost object.

Life-Cycle Costs   Accumulation of costs for activities that occur over the entire life cycle of a product from inception to abandonment.

Process   A series of linked activities that perform a specific objective. A process has a beginning, an end, and clearly identified inputs and outputs.

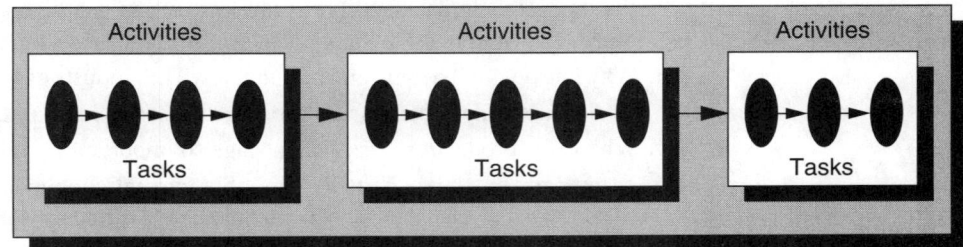

Quality   A customer's total experience with a product or service. It includes features and the performance dimensions of those features such as reliability, usability, safety, and repairability.

Strategy   The way that an organization positions and differentiates itself from its competitors. Positioning refers to the selection of target customers. Distinctions typically are made on the dimensions of quality, cost, and time.

Time   The time it takes a firm to develop and produce new products or to provide existing products when customers need them.

Variable Cost   A cost element that varies directly and proportionately with changes in production volume.

Value Chain   See extended enterprise.

Measuring and Managing Quality Costs

▲ PROBLEMS AND CASES—INTRODUCTORY LEVEL

1. Self-test questions.
  a. What negative impact could result from a lack of quality control in the production processes with regard to an organization's quality strategy?
  b. What negative impact could result from a lack of quality control in the production processes with regard to an organization's cost strategy?
  c. What negative impact could result from a lack of quality control in the production processes with regard to an organization's time-based strategies?
  d. Why has quality become an issue in many U.S. industries?
  e. What statistical properties of a process are used to identify quality problems?
  f. Why is the product/process design stage so important for quality control?
  g. A company purchases parts for assembly into automobile brakes. Identify possible costs related to this activity which could be classified as: 1) prevention, 2) appraisal, 3) internal failure, and 4) external failure costs.
  h. Why must an adequate quality management system go through the six steps outlined in the module?
  i. Why is it important to look at quality costs from a firm-wide perspective and not just at the product or departmental level?
  j. What will be the impact on total costs as a firm moves toward zero defects? Use the cost curves to support your answer.
  k. As a firm moves closer to zero defect, must its prevention and appraisal costs remain at a high level?
  l. Why would a firm choose a six-sigma level of allowable defects rather than a three-sigma level?
  m. Why might a firm choose a three-sigma level of allowable defects rather than a six-sigma level?
  n. If a grocery store found that correct pricing when items are scanned at the cash register has a Value Index of .825 what does this mean? What steps should be taken?
  o. Should a root cause analysis be performed on all problems? What is accomplished by performing a root cause analysis?
  p. How can technical information be used to make decisions regarding quality costs? What are the measurement issues involved in gathering such information?
  q. Can quality costs be determined from an organization's set of traditional financial statements without a special study or reorganization of information? Explain.
  r. Explain how increased visibility of quality costs can cause positive behavioral changes in managers and employees of an organization?
  s. An organization's strategy is to be a low-cost, high-quality producer of lawn mowers. Describe possible design decisions which would support this strategy.
  t. Why might an increase in prevention costs cause a shareholder backlash?
  u. What might managers' reactions be to increases in prevention costs?

2. Visit a local business and identify an individual product or process.

Required:
Determine the following for your selected product or process:

i. Identify inputs (suppliers or previous processes) and outputs (customers or subsequent processes) for the product or process.
ii. Identify what the customer needs are from the outputs.
iii. Identify quality indicators for the product or process.
iv. Choosing one of the quality indicators, identify root causes for sources of variation, problem areas, and opportunities for improvement.
v. Determine costs of quality failure if possible.
vi. Develop workable potential solutions to the problem.

3. The accounting department at a major university recently conducted a survey of its faculty, students, and employers of past graduates on the importance of the various activities performed by the department. The table below shows ten of the activities listed in the survey. The second column shows the current importance ranking that the department places on these activities. The last three columns show the importance rankings generated by the survey. A ranking of one means top priority is assigned to an activity while 10 is the lowest priority.

Survey Results for the Accounting Department

Activity Description	Current Ranking	Faculty Ranking	Student Ranking	Employer Ranking
Providing instruction to student	1	1	1	1
Recruiting new students	2	4	10	3
Establishing and maintaining contact with Big 6 and other CPA firms	3	7	5	4
Hiring, granting tenure, promoting, and dismissing faculty	4	2	7	8
Providing access to computer facilities	5	6	3	2
Updating course curriculum	6	3	8	7
Advising students on courses	7	9	2	9
Advising students on career alternatives	8	8	6	6
Coordinating departmental curriculum with other business courses	9	5	4	5
Providing information on the university procedures and policies	10	10	9	10

Required:
1. Where should quality efforts be concentrated? Since quality is determined from the wants and needs of the customer, who is the customer for the accounting department — is it the students, the faculty, or the employers who will hire the students?
2. How should quality be measured? What areas will require an increase in quality spending? Which area can afford a reduction in quality spending?
3. How can conflicting rankings be handled? Which should receive the most importance — current emphasis, faculty, students, or employers?

4. One of the most prestigious awards given to businesses that demonstrate achievement of a high standard of quality throughout the organization is the Malcolm Baldridge Award. There are many people who doubt that such awards can identify a truly "quality" company. Further, they are skeptical that winning one of these prestigious awards pays off for a company. Many see the pursuit of the award as a public relations avenue for a company, and not as an effort to achieve higher quality.

Required:
1. Use the Internet to investigate the criteria for the Baldridge award. Some Internet sources that would be useful in the research include:

http://davisref.samford.edu/tqm/baldridge.html which describes the past award winners and new award criteria, also http://www.nist.gov/quality_program/doc/95_criteria/1995_AWARD_CRITERIA.html which gives the actual award criteria for 1995. There are also numerous addresses of individual companies and the processes used toward accomplishing the quality necessary to win the award.
2. Argue whether these awards can benefit a company that is striving to increase its quality of output.
3. Indicate how cost information can help in this endeavor.

5. Classify the following costs as prevention, appraisal, internal failure, or external failure.

   i. Certifying vendors as quality suppliers.
   ii. Reinspection of products reworked due to a defect discovered during production.
   iii. Fees for a consultant hired to perform a quality audit.
   iv. Canceled sales orders due to a quality deficiency on a previous shipment to that customer.
   v. Time spent performing a root cause analysis on a defective product.
   vi. Establishing preventive maintenance schedules for equipment.
   vii. Salary for three inspectors to perform final checks before products are shipped to customers.
   viii. Time lost due to work interruptions to correct defects found during inspection.
   ix. Damages paid in a product liability suit.
   x. Altering a production process to reduce worker strain and fatigue.
   xi. Testing of machinery to assure accuracy.
   xii. Formation of "quality circles" for all employees and all departments.

6. The controller of a medium-sized firm that manufactures three styles of metal folding tables has noticed that sales returns and allowances have been increasing over the last several years. While none of the annual increases are material, cumulatively the total percentage of sales returns to sales is becoming significant. The tables are sold in large quantities to schools, convention centers and banquet centers, and to individuals through phone orders from ads placed in the back of home decorating magazines.

Eight hundred and twenty-one tables were returned last year because the customer did not like the product when it arrived (10 percent), defects were found (35 percent), or the wrong table was shipped (55 percent). The controller has decided to begin with the incorrect filling of orders since it is the largest of the three main causes. After questioning the accounting clerk, inventory control manager, and warehouse workers she listed the following information for receiving and reshipping an order.

   i. The accounting clerk spends approximately 10 percent of her time issuing credit memos, replacement invoices, or refund checks. She is paid $6 per hour.
   ii. Tables are sold with a 40 percent markup for large orders and a 60 percent markup for individuals.
   iii. Company policy is to pay the $7.50 per table for return shipping if the return is due to an error on the company's part.
   iv. The inventory control manager spends around five percent of his time updating inventory records for returns. He is paid $9.50 per hour.
   v. A warehouse worker must inspect any returned tables, restock them in the warehouse, and repackage them for future shipment. He is paid $5.50 per hour and estimates that it takes one half hour to perform these tasks for five tables. New shipment cartons are $.60 each.

vi. If more than 30 tables are returned the controller must replan production for the upcoming two-week period. Updates to production schedules are run each Friday and take approximately two hours. The controller earns $65,000 per year.

Required:

1. Calculate the cost of returns due to incorrect filling of orders for the past year.
2. Identify cost differences for individual returns versus institution returns.
3. Identify any additional items that are a result of poor quality in filling orders and has not been included in the cost of returns.

7. Provide an example of a cost that would fall into each of the four quality categories for a manufacturer of T-shirts.

Type of Quality Cost	Cost Description
Prevention	
Appraisal	
Internal failure	
External failure	

8. Mole is a software company that produces leading database software. Programmers write "lines of code" which is tested and shipped to computer and software retail stores for sales to customers. If a software has "bugs," that is, it does not function as desired by customers, it causes various problems such as downtime, loss of data, incorrect results from data sorts, and so on. For each major "bug" identified by customers the company has estimated that it loses 20 percent of its sales for that product. Quality control is currently at three sigma level for detecting bugs in each "module." A typical product has 100 modules. During the last five years sales have declined from $15 million to $12 million due to quality problems.

The company has recently switched to an activity-based accounting system. As part of documenting activities it came across the following tasks that are related to managing software quality. These tasks have been costed but have not been classified to any activities. The costs are shown below.

Activities	Annual Cost 5 Year Average	Last Year
Testing of code lines written by programmers	$150,000	$175,000
Training in latest programming languages	500,000	650,000
Rewriting code that has "bugs"	600,000	1,000,000
Processing software returns from customers	250,000	450,000
Answering telephone queries from customers	250,000	575,000
Installing artificial intelligence software to detect "bugs"	50,000	250,000
Recruiting of trained software engineers	400,000	200,000

Additional Information

Sales revenue	$15,000,000	$12,000,000
Average sale per customer	1,000	700

Required:

1. Classify the activities into the four categories of prevention, appraisal, internal, and external failure.
2. Compute and evaluate spending in the four categories. What does this cost data tell you about how well the company is managing product quality?
3. Assume that increasing to six sigma quality will cost the company $500,000. Is it cost effective for the company to do so? Why? Support your answer with calculations.
4. Assume that an investigation reveals that a key root cause for bugs is hiring of software engineers who did not have adequate training. Evaluate the company's spending on quality relative to this finding.

9. Use the data on quality costs associated with the root cause analysis presented in Exhibit 12 of the module to answer the questions below.

Required:

1. For two of the root causes of customer downtime, paper feed problems and overheating, compute the ratio of failure costs (internal failure and external failure) to non-failure costs (prevention and appraisal).
2. Assume that for these two root causes a 10 percent increase in spending on prevention and appraisal results in a 10 percent decrease in failure costs. If DFP increases its investment in prevention/appraisal by 10 percent, what will be the return (net benefit) on this increased investment? What will be the new ratio of failure costs to non-failure costs?
3. For each of these root causes, compute the return on the increased investment (net reduction in failure costs divided by the increased spending on prevention/appraisal). What conclusion can you draw about the relationship between the failure costs and prevention/appraisal costs and the return on quality spending?

▲ PROBLEMS AND CASES—ADVANCED LEVEL

10. Burnwood Products is a manufacturer of home office and accessory furniture. Products are sold in unassembled kits to discount stores. Last years sales were over $13 million for 21,435 orders. The following information about the production costs was obtained from the accounting records for last year.

Cost Item	Amount
Salaries and wages:	
Design	$210,000
Inspection	28,000
Administration	120,000
Production—regular	630,000
Production—overtime	13,000
Materials and supplies	2,500,000
Consulting fees	33,000
Interview expenses	8,430
Phone system installation	47,500
Utilities and facilities charges	3,727,500
Total	**$7,317,430**

Further analysis revealed the following:

  i. Replacement of defective parts to customers cost $3,240 for the year.
  ii. Burnwood's purchasing and production staff performed a quality audit on the company's 35 suppliers. The audits averaged 10 hours per supplier and the average wage cost was $24 per hour.
  iii. Sixty more candidates were interviewed for the position of operator of the computerized cutting machine than the previous time the position was filled to assure the best possible candidate was found. Each interview costs $45 to perform.
  iv. The phone system was upgraded at a cost of $47,500 during the year to allow the customer service representatives faster response time and better handling of customer calls. These employees earn $7 per hour.
  v. It was estimated that 30 percent of the orders received must be recalculated and the purchaser notified for incorrect prices due to outdated catalogs. Each of these calls takes approximately 15 minutes for the customer service representative.
  vi. In an effort to provide better customer service, the instruction manuals that accompany the furniture kits were lengthened. The additional cost per kit was $1.20 and reduced the number of calls for clarification and reduced frustration on the part of the customer. An outside writer was hired to rewrite the instructions at a cost of $3,500.
  vii. The design of several kits were changed to reduce the number of pieces. The five designers spent two months of their time on these design changes. Designers are paid $42,000 per year.
  viii. One of the $7 per hour production workers is in charge of measuring and charting the defect rate of imperfectly cut pieces. This takes approximately one hour of his time per week.
  ix. Two inspectors are on the staff and are paid $7 per hour. One of the inspectors spends 70 percent of his time inspecting incoming lumber.
  x. A marketing analysis was obtained, at a cost of $33,000, from an outside consultant to determine customer satisfaction and future desires.
  xi. Several furniture kits from a competitor were purchased at a cost of $1,200 to compare to Burnwood's kits. The design staff spent 80 hours assembling and analyzing the kits.
  xii. A quality training program was undertaken with the production staff. After this emphasis on quality, overtime increased by 20 percent in the month following, but then dropped back to normal rates.
  xiii. The final inspection area constitutes 10 percent of the total square feet of the plant.
  xiv. Cost of boards recut due to a miscalculation in measurement was $2,200 during the year.

Required:

1. Determine Burnwood's spending on quality.
2. Classify the quality costs into the categories of prevention, appraisal, internal failure, and external failure.
3. Analyze Burnwood's quality spending. Are they spending enough on quality? Are they concentrating their spending in the right mix between the categories?
4. Design a report for the quality cost information that will allow all employees to understand the impact of poor quality on costs. Keep in mind that most of the employees generally do not receive accounting information and are unfamiliar with traditional accounting terminology.

11. A recent cover story in a national business magazine mentioned the *To The Hilt Hotel* chain (TTH) as an example of how **not** to manage quality. Following the article, TTH hired a consulting firm to recommend ways to improve customer satisfaction. The consultants' study concluded that the factors which determine guests' satisfaction level include the friendliness and efficiency of hotel staff, the attractiveness of the lobby, comfort of beds, and room size. Value Index analysis revealed that TTH was under spending on employee friendliness/efficiency and lobby attractiveness relative to the value placed on these dimensions by hotel guests.

In response to the consultants' recommendation, TTH has decided to experiment with a Total Quality Management program including new training procedures and lobby renovations at its downtown Atlanta hotel, timed to be completed for the heavy tourist traffic expected during the 1996 Summer Olympics. The training is estimated to cost $115,000, and the renovation is estimated to cost $145,000. Last year, 85,000 guests stayed at the hotel.

The consultants' report included the following percentages relating to customer satisfaction:

	Without TQM	With TQM (estimated)
Expectations exceeded	.30	.37
Satisfied	.52	.60
Not satisfied	.18	.03
Estimated new guests	31,000	34,000

Statistics indicate that 80 percent of hotel guests whose expectations are exceeded will return. Of those who are satisfied with their experience, 45 percent will return, and of those who are dissatisfied, only 20 percent will return. Analysis of TTH accounting records indicate that returning guests stay longer, upgrade to higher priced rooms, and require fewer advertising expenses. As a result, the contribution margin per stay (revenue minus cost of servicing the stay) is $41 for returning guests, compared to $39 for new guests.

Required:

1. In analyzing the financial benefit from quality programs, TTH evaluates the return on quality (ROQ), as the net benefit from the program divided by spending required. What is the ROQ of the total quality program recommended by the consultant?
2. Suppose TTH has decided to implement only one quality improvement effort at a time. Based on expected customer satisfaction levels provided by the consultant (below), what will be the ROQ if only the training program is implemented? Only the renovation?

	Training	Renovation
Expectations exceeded	.32	.36
Satisfied	.58	.55
Not satisfied	.10	.09
Estimated new guests	32,000	32,000

3. TTH's Director of Marketing claims it doesn't matter whether TTH undertakes the training program or the renovation, because both will generate the same amount of new business. How would you respond? Use quantitative analysis to support your recommendation.

12. Quality in service after sale is an important part of many businesses that sell products to consumers. The revenues generated on these after-the-sale services can be a substantial part of total revenues. For example, Xerox's service division accounts for 45 percent of the company's gross revenues. When it lost the account to service five printers at the Sprint Corp. headquarters to an independent service organization (ISO) that promised better service, there was much concern.[9] ISOs are a rising industry as customers demand more and better service on the products they buy, and revenue potential of such service increases.

As the controller of a large manufacturer of air conditioning and heating units you are aware that after-the-sale service is important to your business. However, no focus has ever been placed on understanding what after-the-sale service means or the relationship between manufacturing quality and service needs. While the small units sold to individual customers through company-owned dealers are usually only serviced when there is a breakdown or defect, the large units sold to schools, businesses and contractors require annual servicing in addition to breakdown calls. You have become concerned after reading the *Business Week* article and have commissioned a study to investigate how to avoid the loss of this business to ISOs.

Required:
1. How would you define service quality for this type of business?
2. What elements of product quality impact on the need for service?
3. What information relating to cost, quality, or time would help you, the controller, to improve service quality?
4. What behaviors are needed to improve service quality? How can cost of quality data help to generate these behaviors?
5. What kind of organizational culture, values, or mindsets do you need to improve service quality? How can management accounting data help to create or foster a service-oriented organizational culture.

Case 1: Cascade Seating.

Cascade Seating Inc. is a large manufacturer of automobile seat covers. Jan Davis, the controller just received a disturbing call from the plant manager, Dave Garcia. General Motors had just downgraded Cascade from preferred supplier to backup supplier. GM cited the inconsistent fit of the seat covers as the reason, and suggested to Dave that he read an article "How Velcro Got Hooked on Quality."[10] GM had downgraded Velcro a few years back in a similar fashion, but Velcro had managed to turn its quality around and was again a successful preferred supplier to GM.

Jan and Dave immediately got a copy of the article GM had recommended and read it several times through. Both were alarmed at how familiar the story sounded to Cascade and the current situation. Two main points of the article really hit home. Velcro had a quality program in place and thought it was doing well. "We're in the same boat, Dave," Jan said. "We have a quality program which has been showing steady increases in quality for the past two years. But if it's working, then why are we being cited for poor quality products?" "I don't know, Jan, but I know there's another similarity between Velcro and us." Dave went on, "One of GM's big complaints with Velcro was that they were 'inspecting quality in' rather than 'manufacturing quality in.' We work it the same way. We have 15 people assigned to the Quality Control Department right now, and their main task is to be sure that the product going out the door has been inspected. You'll have to ask Ronald,

---
[9] "Slugfest in the Service Biz," *Business Week,* February 28, 1994.
[10] Harvard Business Review, September–October 1989.

the supervisor over there, but I don't see them out on the plant floor working with the production workers, I mostly see them over by finished goods or in their offices."

Jan called a meeting with Dave and the managers of Quality Control, Purchasing, Customer Service, and Inventory Control. As the discussion developed, it became clear that these managers had never met to discuss product quality. Jan listened to each of the managers as they made excuses and pointed fingers at the other departments. "Gentlemen," she finally interrupted, "I don't care about assigning any blame to anyone, and neither does GM. The point here is to figure out where our quality problems lie, and what we can do about them." After that, discussion centered on the problems with quality.

After several hours, the managers concluded that the four main areas of quality problems were in poor quality material, cutting of the material, sewing, or poor inspection. The purchasing manager explained that he spends four hours each month preparing a quality report on the suppliers and performs a yearly review of all suppliers, which takes about 40 hours to complete. Last year he found a new fabric supplier who helped to cut material costs. However, the new supplier's fabric quality was probably not as good as that of his predecessor. As he spoke Jan jotted a note to herself to check the purchasing manager's performance evaluations to see if possibly he was part of the problem as well. She seemed to remember that his evaluations were not very favorable, and that he had not been given a raise above his $22,000 salary.

Dave was unhappy with the cutters and sewers in the plant. Last year the cost of scrapped material was $147,900. Upon investigation he found that 63 percent of the cost for scrapped material was from four cutting related reasons while the other 37 percent was from sewing related reasons. He produced the following data from his files to support this contention:

Reason for scrapping of material	**Percentage of Total**
Cutter cut material incorrectly	28
Cutting machine calibrations off	16
Pattern was incorrect	10
Dull blades on the cutting machine	9
Sewers sewed material incorrectly	25
Sewing machine calibrations off	12

Dave also told the group that when he discovered that the cutting and sewing machine calibrations were incorrect on one of the machines, he had all the cutting and sewing machines checked. This resulted in $5,500 in downtime costs for the cutting machines and $7,400 for the sewing machines. Another $8,200 had been spent last year in rework by the sewers.

At this point the inventory control manager chimed in, "I kept records on the reason for returns last year, and you must do something about your people, Dave. Poor seaming by the sewers accounted for 31 percent of the $56,000 in rejected seat covers by the customer. But the biggest reason for returns, 62 percent, were due to poor fit, most likely due to your cutters not following the patterns correctly. Another seven percent were due to defects in the material. And don't forget about the big shipment of material we returned in October. Around $25,000, as I recall."

Jan was starting to become very dismayed. How could there be quality reports that showed steady increases and yet have all these problems? "Dave, what kind of training takes place for the cutters and sewers?" she finally asked. "Well, cutters go through 40 hours of training, and sewers have six hours. We have 10 cutters, making $7.25 per hour right now, and 36 sewers at $5.50 per hour. My training budget's been cut back so many times that I can't afford to give them any more," he replied. "That's okay, Dave," Jan said, "we're just trying to figure out what our problems are right now, we'll worry about costs and how to solve them later."

Jan next turned to Ronald Fanucci, the manager of the Quality Control Department. He informed her that the quality control procedures had been written four years ago and, except for minor changes, had not been updated since. Further, the procedures had been written primarily by the Quality Control Department with little input from production supervisors. Jan was now quite disturbed. "So where are these 15 people in your department during the day, Ron?" she asked. "Well, three are in incoming inspection, and there's one supervisor over there, and one is in with the pattern making. But the bulk of my staff is in final inspection. I have eight inspectors and one supervisor there." Jan looked at the budget and noted that the inspectors received $12,000 salary per year, the supervisors $18,000 per year, and Ron made $31,000 per year.

As the meeting closed, Jan knew some real progress had been made in determining where the quality problems were. She also knew that there would be a lot of hard work ahead in solving those problems.

Required:
1. Prepare a fishbone diagram, similar to Exhibit 14, identifying the root causes of Cascade Seating's quality problems.
2. Determine the quality costs by category (prevention, appraisal, etc.) and by the performance problems identified in requirement one, similar to Exhibit 12.
3. Why has Cascade run into a quality problem, despite a sizable number of people performing the quality control function?
4. Has the current accounting system helped or hindered the quality efforts?
5. Write a report outlining how Cascade Seating should shift its quality spending to improve product quality?

Case 2: Nuclear Safety Research Inc.

Nuclear Safety Research Inc. (NSR) is a consulting firm which conducts safety examinations of steam tubes in nuclear reactors. Its clients include nuclear power plants throughout the world. In the U.S., most of NSR's clients use what are referred to as "boiling water reactors" (BWR). With all reactors, the steam pipes are one of the more vulnerable points. With boiling water reactors, however, the steam passing through the tubes is radioactive, so the danger is much greater. In addition, the cost of repairs is extremely high, because repairs must be done remotely using sophisticated and expensive robotics equipment. Of approximately 330 reactors world-wide, approximately one-fourth are BWRs. In the U.S., BWRs represent about one third of approximately 110 reactors in use.

The testing procedure to examine steam tubes for flaws and cracks involves using an electronic probe to measure the thickness of the tubing. Under normal conditions, the tubing is the same thickness throughout. Variations in thickness indicate wear, and signal possible future problems. This method is called "nondestructive examination" (NDE), because the tube is left intact. When nondestructive examination indicates a possible defect, the section of tubing is cut out and inspected.

One of NSR's engineers has suggested a way to redesign the electronic probes used in NDEs. The engineering department estimates that redesign of the probes will cost approximately $450,000. NSR's president is intrigued by the idea, since improved accuracy of testing would greatly reduce both cost and risk. He asks Jack Trelligar, NSR's controller, to do a quality cost analysis of probe redesign.

Using normal procedures and existing equipment, NSR's safety review of a reactor takes six to eight months. Of this time, almost two months is preliminary work. First, a schematic diagram of the steam tubes is marked off with a grid, to define sections a few inches square. Testing work is planned so that an examination will be made in each square of the grid. For sections where the risk is higher, such as where the tube attaches to nozzles or flanges, a finer grid is used, and test readings are closer together.

NSR routinely monitors equipment reliability in its testing lab by taking readings of sample tubes, some of which are known to have defects. In addition, NSR routinely re-tests some tubes examined in the field. Last year, the firm completed NDE engagements at 57 nuclear power plants world-wide, and examined a total of 969,000 steam tubes. Of these, the firm re-analyzed 226,500 tests. Re-tests found erroneous test results in 679 cases.

Two types of errors may occur in testing. A *false positive* occurs when test results identify the tube as defective, but there is in fact no flaw in the tube. A *false negative* results when the tube passes inspection, but there is in fact a crack or hole (see Exhibit 15). A false positive is expensive for the client firm, because cutting the tube section open disrupts operations. A false negative, however, is far more dangerous.

Exhibit 15
Types of Testing Errors

Actual Condition of Tube	Test Result — Defective	Test Result — Not Defective
Defective	True positive	False negative
Not defective	False positive	True negative

At the client facility, there is no way to know when a false negative has occurred. This is particularly dangerous, since the Nuclear Regulatory Commission routinely extends licenses of facilities which receive clean test results for an additional 20 years beyond the normal 40-year life of a reactor. This means tubes are operated well beyond the intended life, and the danger of an accident is greatly increased. Recently, based on the results of NSR's tests, a client facility was shut down and all 17,000 steam tubes were repaired, at a cost of $40 million.

Required:

1. Is NSR operating at three-sigma quality levels or six-sigma levels?
2. When a test of steam tubes at a client facility produces a *false positive* result, what activities will NSR perform? What activities will the client perform? How would you estimate the costs of these activities?
3. When a test of steam tubes at a client facility produces a *false negative* result, what activities will NSR perform? What activities will the client perform? How would you estimate the costs of these activities?
4. Do you think the probe should be redesigned? With so little cost data available, how can the firm analyze this decision?
5. Should the firm go to six-sigma quality levels? Will this decision be cost effective or is it likely to show diminishing returns at some point?
6. One of the firm's major markets is developing countries, where the availability of low-cost electricity generated by nuclear power plants makes economic development possible. The citizens of these countries rely on subsistence agriculture which has resulted in soil depletion, desalination, and "desertification" making life increasingly difficult. Would you advocate a six-sigma quality level if these countries are willing to certify a plan at the current three-sigma level?

NOTES

NOTES

NOTES

NOTES

NOTES

NOTES

NOTES

LIST OF MODULES

MANAGEMENT ACCOUNTING—A STRATEGIC FOCUS, A MODULAR SERIES

Currently Available:

Strategy and Management Accounting
Management Accounting in the Age of Lean Production
Target Costing
Measuring and Managing Environmental Costs
Measuring and Managing Quality Costs
Activity Based Management
Measuring and Managing Capacity
Measuring and Managing Indirect Costs
Manufacturing Overhead Allocation: Traditional and Activity Based
The Organizational Role of Management Accountants

Forthcoming Modules:

Strategic Budgeting Part I: The Annual Profit and Cash Budget
The Kaleidoscopic Nature of Costs: Cost Terms and Classifications
An Overview of Cost Measurement Systems
International Managerial Accounting
Measuring and Managing Time to Market
Theory of Constraints
Managing Supply Chain and Make or Buy Decisions
Benchmarking for Competitor and Value Chain Analysis
Activity Based Marketing and Distribution Cost Analysis
Cost Management Using Business Process Reengineering
Cost Analysis for Pricing and Capacity Use Decisions
Cost Profit Product Mix and Volume Analysis
Product Costing in Mass Manufacturing-Process Costing
Job Costing in Mass and Lean Manufacturing Environments
Product Costing in Lean Manufacturing-Operations Costing
Joint Cost Problems in Manufacturing and Service Industries
Strategic Budgeting Part II: Multi-year Product and Profit Planning
Strategic Budgeting Part III: Long-term Capital Budgeting
Customer Profitability Analysis
Driver Based Cost Estimation Methods
Experience Based Cost Estimation Methods
Standard and Kaizen Costing
Variance Analysis
Analyzing Throughout, Mix and Yield
Inventory Management in Mass and Lean Environments
Capacity Rationing Using Linear Programming
The Historical Evolution of Cost Accounting
Absorption Cost vs. Variable Cost Systems
Management Accounting Systems and Information Technology
Measuring Preproduction Costs

PRICING AND PACKAGING

Following is the updated pricing schedule for the series, effective January 1, 1997. (REMEMBER: Any combination of modules may be ordered and the STRATEGY AND MANAGEMENT module is always included for FREE.)

1. The net price for any individual module is $6.00.
2. For orders between 2 and 5 modules, the net price per module is $6.00.
3. For orders between 6 and 10 modules, the net price per module is $5.00.
4. For orders between 11 and 15 modules, the net price per module will be $4.00.
5. For orders of 16 or more modules, the net price per module will be $3.50.

We have established a sliding scale designed to offer discounts as more modules are used. Our pricing scale is competitive with textbook prices.